CHRISTMAS

DENNY ROBSON

FRANKLIN WATTS
LONDON · NEW YORK · TORONTO · SYDNEY

CONTENTS

Design: David West
              Children's Book Design
Designer: Flick Killerby
Photography: Roger Vlitos

© Aladdin Books Ltd 1992

Created and designed by
N.W. Books Ltd
28 Percy Street
London W1P 9FF

First published in
Great Britain in 1992 by
Franklin Watts Ltd
96 Leonard Street
London EC2A 4RH

ISBN 07496 07866

A CIP catalogue record for this book
is available from the British Library

Printed in Belgium

Introduction

Christmas is an exciting time — nativity plays at school, carol services to celebrate the birth of Jesus, trees to decorate, stockings to be hung up, cards and presents to be exchanged, as well as all the fun to be had with your friends and family.

You can also have a lot of fun with the preparations and this book is full of ideas to help you get ready for Christmas. There are cards for you to make, an advent calendar, hanging decorations, baubles for the tree, wrapping papers and even a nativity scene.

Some of the ideas are simple and can be made quite quickly. Others will take more time and you may need the help of an older person. But they are all great fun and they should get you into the festive spirit!

Here are some of the materials used to make the projects in this book. Most things are not expensive to buy and you may find much of what you need at home. (This Christmas, remember to save a few cards to be used in your preparations for next year.) Before you begin, check the materials needed and gather everything together. It's also a good idea to cover your work surface with newspaper before you begin.

Christmas cards

Your Christmas greetings to friends and family will be even more special if you send them on home-made cards. Try these designs and then see if you can make up others of your own.

You will need thin card, scissors, felt pens, coloured tissue paper, foil, glitter, glue, gummed stars.

1 To make the snowman and stocking, fold the card, draw the shapes and cut them out from the fold so that the shapes are double. Draw the robin on single card and cut out.

1

2

2 Decorate your cards as shown. When using glitter, first fold and unfold a piece of paper and place this under the card. You can then refold the paper and pour any excess glitter back into the tube.

5

When you open this card, the partridge pops out of the pear tree!

1 Fold the card in two. Trace one of the shapes shown on the folded edge and cut along the solid lines. Now fold this section in along the dotted lines. This is the inside of the card.

1

2

2 Decorate the inside. Fold another piece of card of the same size. This is the outside of the card. Decorate the front. Cut out the partridge.

3

3 Stick the partridge onto the pop-out section, making sure that it will fold into the card.

In this card, Santa's sleigh flies through the night sky, leaving a trail of stars.

1 Take three pieces of card the same size. Paint two blue as shown. Cut a window in the top card and stick a trail of stars to the base in the same position.

2 Draw your Santa on a strip of card a little longer than the window.

3 Trace the window onto the third piece of card. Cut it out to one edge and glue to the base card. This acts as a runner to keep Santa in place.

4 Slide the strip into the base.

5 Glue the top to the base.

Garlands

Paper chains and garlands are very traditional Christmas decorations. They can be hung diagonally across a room, or strung along the walls to make your home look festive. They can be as long as you want, (unlike the ones in the shops!), and are very simple to make.

You will need coloured paper, pencil, ruler, scissors, stapler, glue.

1 For the square garland, take lots of squares of coloured paper and cut out a smaller square from each, leaving a border of about 3cm.

2 Staple together so that the first square is stapled to the second at the corners of one diagonal. Then take the other diagonal on the second square and staple this to the third square, and so on.

1 To make the paper chain garland, cut lots of strips of coloured paper, each about 3cm x 20cm. Roll the first strip into a circle and glue the edges together.

2 Link another strip through the first and glue the edges. Continue linking the strips, alternating the colours, until the chain is as long as you want it to be.

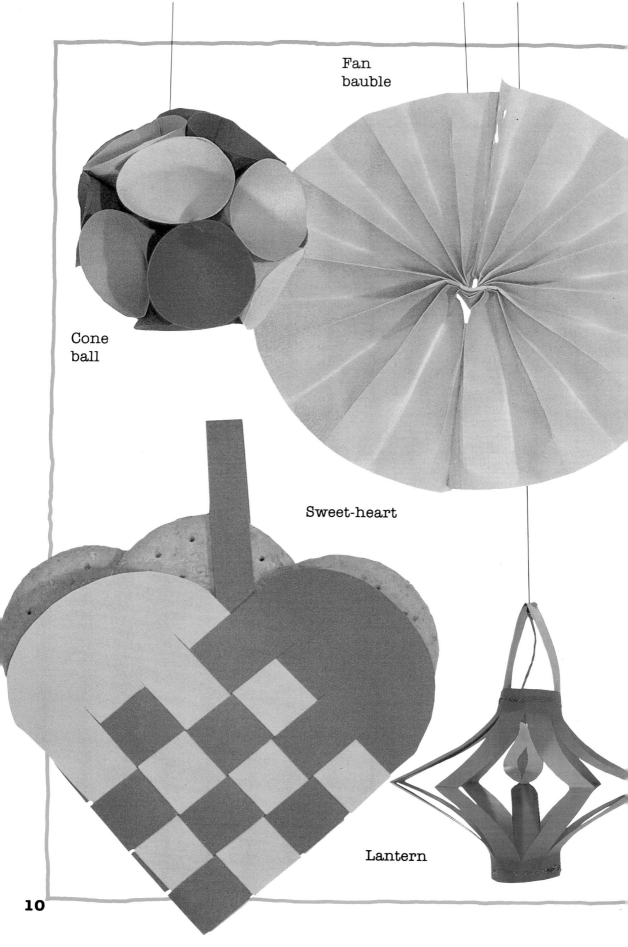

Fan
bauble

Cone
ball

Sweet-heart

Lantern

10

Tree decorations

For many people, Christmas wouldn't be Christmas without a tree decorated with fairy lights, tinsel and baubles. Here are some ideas for decorations that could be hung from the tree, or from the ceiling. Decorate with paints or glitter to make them even more special. You can find out how to make an angel to go on top of the tree on page 30.

You will need coloured paper, glue, glitter, biscuits or sweets to put in the sweet-heart basket, ribbon or string for hanging.

1

1 To make the cone ball, cut out twelve circles of coloured paper and then cut each circle in half. Glue along the straight edges and roll them into cones.

2 Mixing the colours, glue all the cones together so that they form a ball. Attach ribbon or string with sticky tape and then hang the decoration on the tree.

2

1 To make the fan bauble, first take a sheet of coloured paper. Fold the paper backwards and forwards several times so that it makes pleats.

1

2 Fold the pleated paper in half and then glue the edges together as shown.

2

1 This lantern looks really effective, yet it's quick and easy to make. First fold a sheet of coloured paper in half.

1

1 To make the sweet-heart, take two pieces of paper 6 by 20cm of different colours. Fold in half across the width and cut a curve opposite the fold. Make three cuts from the fold as shown.

1

2 Interweave the two parts together and the heart will open out to make a basket.

2

3

2 Make cuts along the folded edge.

3 Open out and glue along the two long sides.

4 Glue a paper strip to your lantern to make a handle. Cut out the paper candle and attach it to the handle using sticky tape and string.

2

4

'Stained glass' pictures

Have you noticed the stained glass windows in some churches? Here is an idea for a 'stained glass' Christmas picture for you to make. The design can be as simple as you like — a big star or an arched window, for example. Or you can trace a picture with lots of detail, like this decorated Christmas tree and presents. When it's finished, hang your picture up against a window so that the light shines through the coloured paper.

You will need black card, pencil, coloured tissue paper, tracing paper for more detailed designs, glue, scissors.

1

1 For simple designs, draw directly onto the black card with a light-coloured pencil. Use tracing paper to copy more detailed designs.

2 If tracing, transfer the design to the card. Go over the outlines if necessary.

2

3 Carefully cut out the shapes. You may need the help of an adult. Make sure that the card between the spaces is not too thin or it will tear.

4 Glue coloured tissue to one side of the card so that the cut out shapes are completely covered.

Advent calendar

Count down the days to Christmas with this advent calendar. Behind each 'window' draw a Christmas picture – an angel, star, Christmas tree, presents, baubles, holly or a snowman, for example. For the 24 December, you could make a bigger window and draw the baby Jesus in a manger. Open the first window on 1 December and continue opening a window each day until you get to Christmas Day. Then pull Santa down the chimney!

You will need card, tracing paper, paints or felt pens, black paper, glue.

1

1 Draw the design onto card, or if you prefer, experiment on tracing paper first and then transfer to the card.

2

2 Draw Santa on a separate piece of card as shown. Mark 24 windows. Colour in your picture with paints or felt pens.

3 Cut out three sides of each window. Glue the edges of the picture to a piece of card of the same size. Draw small pictures behind each window.

3

4

4 Cut a slit along the chimney through both pieces of card. Push Santa up the chimney.

5

5 Turn the picture over and glue a piece of card around Santa to keep him in place.

Glue   Back of Santa

6

6 When all the windows have been opened and it's Christmas Day, pull Santa down the chimney!

Christmas crackers

Crackers for the dinner table can make your Christmas meals go with a bang! Here is a design for a very easy cracker to make yourself. You can fill it with anything you want, sweets, small toys, party hats, jokes or mottos. Make each one different for the different members of your family. Decorate the crackers with small pictures cut from old Christmas cards.

You will need coloured tissue paper, coloured crêpe paper, a cardboard roll for each cracker, sweets or small toys, jokes or mottos, glue, scissors.

1 Make a party hat to go into each cracker. Cut a strip of tissue paper about 12cm wide. It should be long enough to fit around the head of the person who will wear it, plus a little over to overlap and glue.

2 Fold the strip into wide pleats and cut out a triangle from the top.

3 Unfold the strip and glue the ends together. You could decorate the hats with glitter or gummed shapes.

1 To make the crackers, first cut each cardboard roll at the centre. Make a jagged rather than a straight cut and then fit the rolls back together.

1

2 Wrap each roll in a piece of crêpe paper. The paper must be wide enough to twist the ends.

3

2

3 Twist one end of the cracker and fill it with sweets, hat, jokes etc. Twist up the other end and then decorate the cracker.

Wrapping paper

Giving and receiving presents is one of the nicest things about Christmas, and your presents will look even more special if you make your own wrapping paper. Here are two kinds of paper for you to make, one patterned with potato prints and the other marbled. Use poster paint for the prints, but for the marbled paper you will need to use oil paints thinned with white spirit.

You will need large sheets of plain paper, poster paints, oil paints thinned with white spirit, (ask an adult to help), potatoes, felt pen, knife, bowl of water.

1 Cut the potatoes in half.

1

2 Draw a simple design onto the cut surfaces of each potato.

2

3 Carefully cut around each design so that it stands out. You may need the help of an adult for this.

3

4 Dip the potato shapes into poster paints and print all over the paper. Leave it to dry.

4

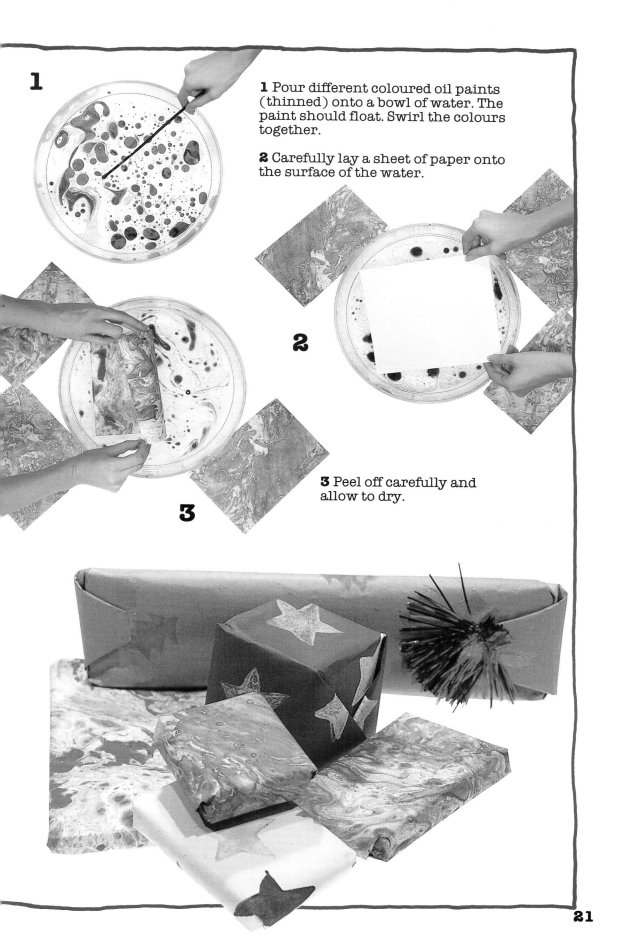

1 Pour different coloured oil paints (thinned) onto a bowl of water. The paint should float. Swirl the colours together.

2 Carefully lay a sheet of paper onto the surface of the water.

3 Peel off carefully and allow to dry.

Snowflake mobile

This snowflake mobile looks pretty hanging in the hall or stairwell where it can catch the air movements. You may have to experiment when putting it all together so that it hangs balanced. Real snowflake crystals all have six points, but you can make your snowflakes as varied as you like. They also make pretty decorations if you stick them to the windows.

You will need squares of paper for the snowflakes, thin card for the cloud, cotton wool balls, thread, scissors, sticky tape, glue.

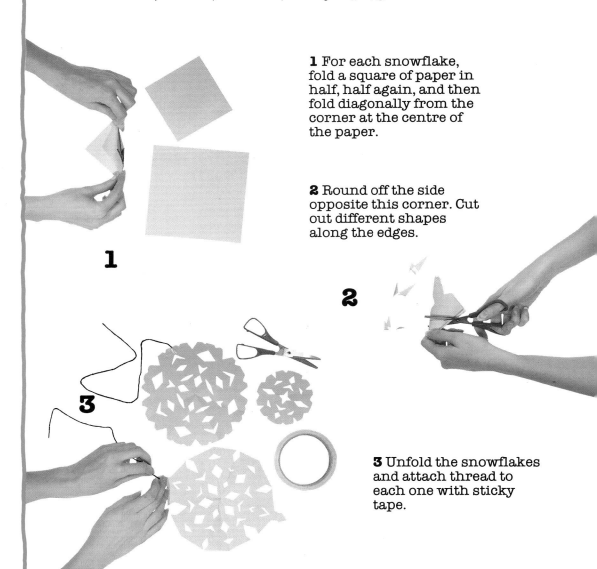

1 For each snowflake, fold a square of paper in half, half again, and then fold diagonally from the corner at the centre of the paper.

2 Round off the side opposite this corner. Cut out different shapes along the edges.

3 Unfold the snowflakes and attach thread to each one with sticky tape.

4

4 Cut the cloud from thin card and stick the snowflakes' threads to the back, at different heights.

5

5 Glue cotton wool balls to the front of the cloud.

6 Hang up the mobile and watch the snowflakes sway in the breeze.

6

Snowstorm

Even if you have no snow at Christmas, you can still create your own snowstorm in a jar. This carol singer caught in the snow is fun to make. You could design lots of different characters and give them as presents to your friends.

You will need a glass jar with a tight-fitting lid, water, tinsel or kitchen foil for the snow, different coloured plasticine, a pencil.

1 Make the carol singer's body from plasticine. Give him a scarf and two arms. Fix two mittens to his book of carols and attach to his arms.

2 Roll a ball of plasticine for his head, attach a 'woolly' hat, two eyes and a cold red nose.

3 Use the point of a pencil to make his singing mouth.

3

4 Put a base of plasticine on the jar lid and fix the carol singer *firmly* to it.

4

5

5 Fill the jar with water and add strands cut from a piece of tinsel, or tiny pieces of kitchen foil. Screw on the lid tightly and shake the jar to see the snow swirl.

Gift boxes

Here are some pretty Christmas gift boxes for you to make. You can make them any size you like and fill them with sweets or presents to give to your friends and family. Decorate them with glitter, gummed shapes and pictures, or you can print them with the potato cuts as you did with the wrapping paper. The design for each box is on page 32.

You will need thin card, pencil and ruler, glue, glitter, gummed shapes, paints or potato shapes to decorate.

1 Copy shape 1 shown on page 32 with a pencil and ruler. Draw in the dotted lines and cut along the solid lines. The box can be as large as you like, but you may need the help of an adult to work out the size.

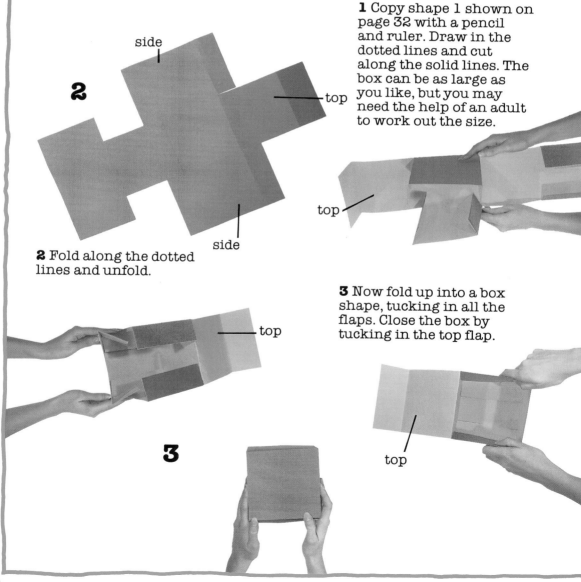

side

top

2

top

side

2 Fold along the dotted lines and unfold.

3 Now fold up into a box shape, tucking in all the flaps. Close the box by tucking in the top flap.

top

3

top

1 Copy shape 2 on page 32 and cut out twice, making one shape slightly larger than the other. This will be the lid of the box. (Again, you may need the help of an adult to work out the size.)

1

2 Fold up along the dotted lines. Fold in the tabs and glue them to the sides.

2

3 Decorate your boxes and fill them with sweets or presents.

3

Nativity scene

Here are some ideas for a nativity scene for you to make. A bright new star twinkles in the sky above the stable where Jesus has just been born. Mary and Joseph stand beside him in the stable. An angel has appeared to tell the shepherds about Jesus' birth and they have come to visit. Three kings have also followed the star, bringing gifts for the baby Jesus.

You will need card, a shoe box, a match box for the crib, straw or yellow wool, gold foil, gummed stars, paints and paint brush, tissue and crêpe paper, cotton wool, pipe cleaners, tinsel, glue.

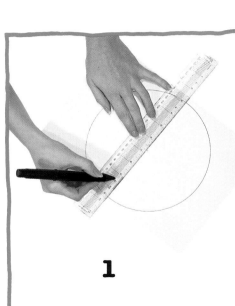

1 Draw a circle on card using a plate or saucer. (Do this for as many characters as you need.) Draw a line through the middle.

2 Using a cotton reel, draw the head as shown. Cut out the semi-circle with head.

1

2

3 Roll each body into a cone shape. Glue the edges together.

3

Angel

4 The angel has a tunic and arms made of white paper, and a gold foil halo and wings.

4

5 Glue semi-circles of tissue or crêpe paper around the figures to make the clothes. Attach card arms.

5

6 Decorate the figures as you like. The three kings can have tinsel or glitter crowns.

6

Baby Jesus

1 For the baby Jesus, wind half a pink pipe cleaner into a flat circle for the head.

2 Coil two others around the other half to make the body. Make sure you have two arms and two legs. Use white tissue for his clothes.

Sheep

1 Curl the end of a white pipe cleaner to make the sheep's head. Now curve the pipe cleaner so that the cotton ball will fit into it.

2 Twist two black pipe cleaners around the frame for legs. Push a strip of black paper through the head for ears.

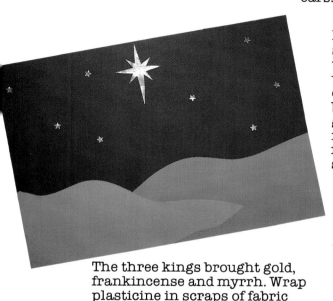

For the backdrop to the scene, you could paint the sky and hills onto white card or stick coloured paper onto black card. Stick gummed stars on the night sky and make a big foil star to go over the stable.

The three kings brought gold, frankincense and myrrh. Wrap plasticine in scraps of fabric and tie with tinsel, and make a 'chest' of gold foil as your gifts.

Gift box designs

Copy these designs to make the Christmas gift boxes on page 26. The boxes can be made to any size you wish. You may need the help of a grownup to calculate the scale.

1

2

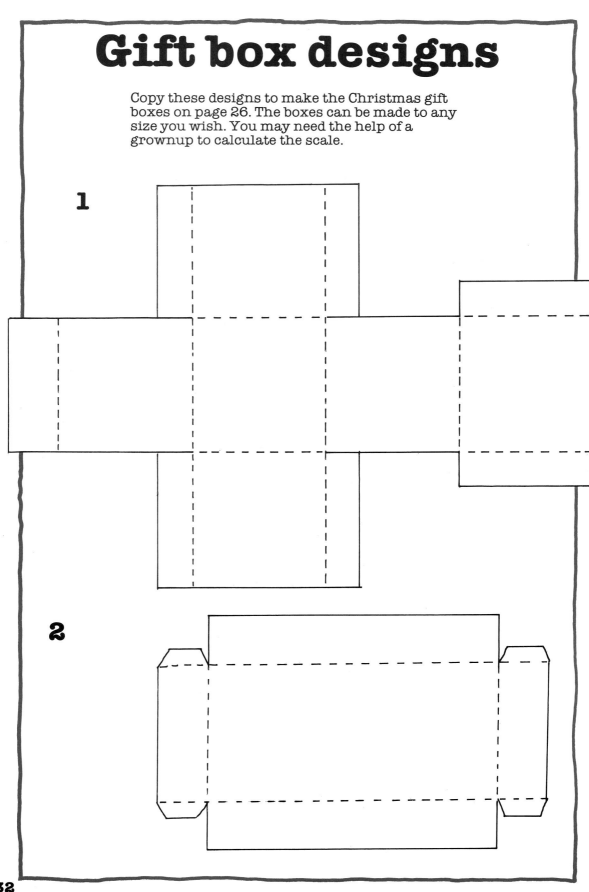